PIANO • VOCAL • GUITAR

# COUNTRY SUPERSTARS OF THE 90'S

| | | |
|---|---|---|
| 2 | Back In My Younger Days | Don Williams |
| 7 | Born To Be Blue | The Judds |
| 14 | Chasin' That Neon Rainbow | Alan Jackson |
| 26 | Come Next Monday | K.T. Oslin |
| 21 | Fast Movin' Train | Restless Heart |
| 32 | Friends In Low Places | Garth Brooks |
| 38 | Ghost In This House | Shenandoah |
| 48 | Help Me Hold On | Travis Tritt |
| 42 | Here's A Quarter (Call Someone Who Cares) | Travis Tritt |
| 55 | I Couldn't See You Leavin' | Conway Twitty |
| 60 | I Meant Every Word He Said | Ricky Van Shelton |
| 68 | I've Come To Expect It From You | George Strait |
| 64 | I've Cried My Last Tear For You | Ricky Van Shelton |
| 78 | It Ain't Nothin' | Keith Whitley |
| 82 | Love Without End, Amen | George Strait |
| 88 | Lucky Moon | Oak Ridge Boys |
| 94 | On Second Thought | Eddie Rabbitt |
| 73 | Rumor Has It | Reba McEntire |
| 98 | She Came From Fort Worth | Kathy Mattea |
| 103 | Time Passes By | Kathy Mattea |
| 106 | Wanted | Alan Jackson |
| 112 | Who's Lonely Now | Highway 101 |
| 118 | You Know Me Better Than That | George Strait |
| 123 | You Lie | Reba MacEntire |

36 ONTARIO ST.
STRATFORD, ONT.
N5A 3G8
(519) 271-9102

**Hal Leonard Publishing Corporation**
7777 West Bluemound Road P.O. Box 13819 Milwaukee, WI 53213

ISBN 0-7935-1109-7

# BACK IN MY YOUNGER DAYS

Words and Music by
DANNY FLOWERS

Oh, it does-n't seem that _

long a - go. _ You, _____

you make it feel _ like the first time we made _ love, _____ and I ain't

ev - er get-tin' e - nough. _ Well, _ well, well. _____

young - er days \_\_\_\_

It's bet - ter than it

used to be \_\_\_\_

back in my young - er days. \_

**Repeat and Fade**

# BORN TO BE BLUE

Words and Music by BRENT MAHER,
MIKE REID and MACK DAVID

MCA music publishing

**D.S. al Coda**

They say no -

**CODA**

A7

Was I born ___ to be blue, born ___ just to cry, Born ___ to be a - lone 'till the day I die?

# CHASIN' THAT NEON RAINBOW

Words and Music by JIM McBRIDE
and ALAN JACKSON

"Son, I just know we're gon-na hear you sing-in' on it some-day."

Well, I ___ made it up to Mu - sic Row, ___ but

Lord - y, don't the wheels_ turn_ slow. Still, I would-n't trade a min-ute; I

would-n't have it an - y oth-er way. ___ Just show me to the stage,_ I'm ___

# FAST MOVIN' TRAIN

Words and Music by
DAVE LOGGINS

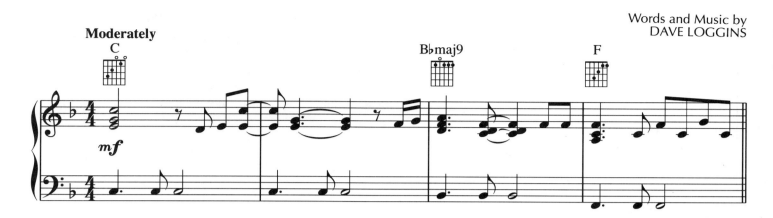

She had a long line of lov-ers, __
I had a weak-ness for her __ kind of wom-an
I won-dered as I lay there and held her

most-ly the gam-blin' __ kind.
I could nev-er de-ny. __
why can't this be real.

I did-n't want to
I knew I would-n't
And why the fear

mov - in' __ train.

D.S. al Coda
(Take 2nd ending)

CODA

- er ____ fast __ mov - in' train.

Repeat and Fade

*Instrumental*

# COME NEXT MONDAY

Words and Music by K.T. OSLIN,
RORY MICHAEL BOURKE and CHARLIE BLACK

# FRIENDS IN LOW PLACES

Words and Music by DEWAYNE BLACKWELL
and EARL BUD LEE

a - way and I'll be o - kay.

Yeah, I'm not big___ on so - cial grac - es. Think I'll

slip on___ down___ to the o - a - sis. Oh,___ I've got friends___

**Repeat and Fade**

in low_____ plac - es. ___

# GHOST IN THIS HOUSE

Words and Music by
HUGH PRESTWOOD

# HERE'S A QUARTER
## (CALL SOMEONE WHO CARES)

Words and Music by
TRAVIS TRITT

# HELP ME HOLD ON

Words and Music by TRAVIS TRITT
and PAT TERRY

Ba - by close _ that suit - case you been pack- - ing. _ Just sit down _ and talk _ to me _ a while. _ I know you tried to tell _ me what was lack - ing, _ but I guess _

# I COULDN'T SEE YOU LEAVIN'

Words and Music by RONNY SCAIFE
and RORY MICHAEL BOURKE

# I MEANT EVERY WORD HE SAID

Words and Music by CURLY PUTMAN,
BUCKY JONES and JOE CHAMBERS

62

# I'VE CRIED MY LAST TEAR FOR YOU

Words and Music by CHRIS WATERS
and TONY KING

# I'VE COME TO EXPECT IT FROM YOU

Words and Music by DEAN DILLON
and BUDDY CANNON

**Moderate Two-Beat**

1. So up - set,
2. A mil - lion times,
3. *Instrumental*
4. I could raise hell,

A nerv - ous wreck. can't be - lieve you said good - bye.
A mil - lion lines and I bought 'em ev - 'ry - one.
But what the hell, it would - n't do a bit of good.

# RUMOR HAS IT

Words and Music by LARRY SHELL,
VERN DANT and BRUCE BURCH

74

# IT AIN'T NOTHIN'

Words and Music by
TONY HASELDEN

# LOVE WITHOUT END, AMEN

Words and Music by
AARON G. BARKER

# LUCKY MOON

Words and Music by DOUG JOHNSON
and MARK WRIGHT

# ON SECOND THOUGHT

**Moderately Bright Shuffle**

Words and Music by
EDDIE RABBITT

Some - times __ a man does
I know __ it's not __ your fault __

*Instrumental*

things with - out __ half think - ing, __ and
that you're __ so __ pret - ty, __ and

what I saw __ I did __ not un - der - stand. __
that you turn __ the head __ of ev - 'ry man. __ I un - der -

__ sec - ond thought, __ I'll just turn a - round __ here in my tracks __

__ and walk back __ in - to your arms __ where I be - long. __

__ I was wrong. On sec - ond thought,

I a - pol - o - gize __ for what I've done, __ 'cause you're the on -

# SHE CAME FROM FORT WORTH

Words and Music by FRED KOLLER
and PAT ALGER

# TIME PASSES BY

Words and Music by JON VEZNER
and SUSAN LONGACRE

do what __ we like __ and love while __ we're here _____ be - fore __

time pass - es __ by.

To Coda ⊕

D.S. al Coda

CODA ⊕

# WANTED

Words and Music by CHARLIE CRAIG
and ALAN JACKSON

# WHO'S LONELY NOW

**Moderate Country two beat**

Words and Music by KIX BROOKS
and DON COOK

Lyrics (verse 1 / verse 2):

You walked out on a good love._____ You found some‐bod‐y new._____

I feel a whole lot bet‐ter._____ I've got a new at‐ti‐tude._____

See your local music dealer for a complete selection of
Hal Leonard music books or

# Send for a free catalog:

☐ PIANO AND ORGAN

☐ ELECTRONIC KEYBOARDS

☐ GUITAR, BASS & OTHER
FRETTED INSTRUMENTS

Name _____

Address _____

City _____ State _____ Zip _____ CCA

**Hal Leonard Publishing Corporation**

7777 West Bluemound Road P.O. Box 13819 Milwaukee, WI 53213

PLACE
STAMP
HERE

114

# YOU KNOW ME BETTER THAN THAT

By TONY HASELDEN
and ANNA LISA GRAHAM

# YOU LIE

Words and Music by AUSTIN ROBERTS,
BOBBY FISCHER and CHARLIE BLACK

We lie in the dark. __ I
Des - p'rate to talk, __
How long un - til __ you

know you're a - wake. __ The on - ly sounds __ are the
yearn - ing to touch, __ burn - ing in - side __ 'cause I
just can't go __ on, and the urge to break __ loose is

# *Your Favorites in* COUNTRY MUSIC *and more...*

**#1 COUNTRY SONGS OF THE 80'S**
44 Chart-topping country hits, including: American Made • Any Day Now • Could I Have This Dance • Crying My Heart Out Over You • Forever And Ever Amen • Forty Hour Week (For A Livin') • Grandpa (Tell Me 'Bout The Good Old Days) • He Stopped Loving Her Today • I Was In The Stream • My Heroes Have Always Been Cowboys • Smoky Mountain Rain • Why Not Me • You're The Reason God Made Oklahoma.
_____00360715    $12.95

**80'S LADIES—TOP HITS FROM COUNTRY WOMEN OF THE 80'S**
23 songs by today's female country stars including: Roseanne Cash, Crystal Gayle, The Judds, Reba McEntire, Anne Murray, K.T. Oslin and others. Songs include: I Don't Know Why You Don't Want Me • Lyin' In His Arms Again • Why Not Me • A Sunday Kind Of Love • Could I Have This Dance • Do'Ya • Strong Enough To Bend.
_____00359741    $9.95

**THE AWARD-WINNING SONGS OF THE COUNTRY MUSIC ASSOCIATION  First Edition**
All of the official top five songs nominated for the CMA "Song Of The Year" from 1967 to 1983. 85 selections, featuring: Always On My Mind • Behind Closed Doors • Don't It Make My Brown Eyes Blue • Elvira • The Gambler • I.O.U. • Mammas Don't Let Your Babies Grow Up To Be Cowboys • Swingin' • You're The Reason God Made Oklahoma.
_____00359485    $16.95

**AWARD-WINNING SONGS OF THE COUNTRY MUSIC ASSOCIATION Second Edition**
An update to the first edition, this songbook features 18 songs nominated for "Song of the Year" by the Country Music Association from 1984 through 1987. Songs include: Islands In The Stream • To All The Girls I've Loved Before • God Bless The U.S.A. • Seven Spanish Angels • Grandpa (Tell Me 'Bout The Good Old Days) • On The Other Hand • All My Ex's Live In Texas • Forever And Ever, Amen.
_____00359486    $8.95

**THE NEW ULTIMATE COUNTRY FAKE BOOK**
More than 700 of the greatest country hits of all-time. Includes an alphabetical index and an artist index! Includes: Cold, Cold Heart • Crazy • Crying My Heart Out Over You • Daddy Sang Bass • Diggin' Up Bones • God Bless The U.S.A. • Grandpa (Tell Me 'Bout The Good Old Days) • Great Balls Of Fire • Green, Green Grass Of Home • He Stopped Loving Her Today • I.O.U. • I Was Country When Country Wasn't Cool • I Wouldn't Have Missed It For The World • Lucille • Mammas Don't Let Your Babies Grow Up To Be Cowboys • On The Other Hand • Ruby, Don't Take Your Love To Town • Swingin' • Talking In Your Sleep • Through The Years • Whoever's In New England • Why Not Me • You Needed Me • and MORE!
_____00240049    $35.00

**THE BEST COUNTRY SONGS EVER**
We've updated this outstanding collection of country songs to include even more of your favorites—over 75 in all! Featuring: Always On My Mind • Behind Closed Doors • Could I Have This Dance • Crazy • Daddy Sang Bass • D-I-V-O-R-C-E • Forever And Ever, Amen • God Bless The U.S.A. • Grandpa (Tell Me 'Bout The Good Old Days) • Help Me Make It Through The Night • I Fall To Pieces • If We Make It Through December • Jambalaya (On The Bayou) • Love Without End, Amen • Mammas Don't Let Your Babies Grow Up To Be Cowboys • Stand By Your Man • Through The Years • and more. Features stay-open binding.
_____00359135    $15.95

**THE GREAT AMERICAN COUNTRY SONGBOOK**
The absolute best collection of top country songs anywhere. 70 titles, featuring: Any Day Now • Could I Have This Dance • Heartbroke • I Was Country When Country Wasn't Cool • I'm Gonna Hire A Wino To Decorate Our Home • It's Hard To Be Humble • Jambalaya • Smokey Mountain Rain • Through The Years • many others.
_____00359947    $12.95

**COUNTRY LOVE SONGS**
25 Sentimental country favorites, including: Could I Have This Dance • Forever And Ever, Amen • She Believes In Me • Through The Years • The Vows Go Unbroken • You Decorated My Life • You Needed Me • and more.
_____00311528    $9.95

**COUNTRY STANDARDS**
A collection of 51 of country's biggest hits, including: (Hey Won't You Play) Another Somebody Done Somebody Wrong Song • By The Time I Get To Phoenix • Could I Have This Dance • Daddy Sang Bass • Forever And Ever, Amen • Bless The U.S.A. • Green, Green Grass Of Home • Islands In The Stream • King Of The Road • Little Green Apples • Lucille • Mammas Don't Let Your Babies Grow Up To Be Cowboys • Ruby Don't Take Your Love To Town • Stand By Me • Through The Years • Your Cheatin' Heart.
_____00359517    $10.95

**COUNTRY MUSIC HALL OF FAME**
The Country Music Hall Of Fame Was Founded in 1961 by the Country Music Association (CMA). Each Year, new members are elected—and these books are the first to represent all of its members with photos, biography and music selections related to each individual.

**Volume 1**
Includes: Fred Rose, Hank Williams, Jimmie Rodgers, Roy Acuff, George D. Hay, PeeWee King, Minnie Pearl and Grandpa Jones. 23 songs, including: Blue Eyes Crying In The Rain • Cold, Cold Heart • Wabash Cannon Ball • Tennesse Waltz.
_____00359510    $8.95

**Volume 2**
Features: Tex Ritter, Ernest Tubb, Eddy Arnold, Jim Denny, Joseph Lee Frank, Uncle Dave Macon, Jim Reeves and Bill Monroe. Songs include: Jealous Heart • Walking The Floor Over You • Make The World Go Away • Ruby, Don't Take Your Love To Town • Kentucky Waltz • Is It Really Over • many more.
_____00359504    $8.95

**Volume 3**
Red Foley, Steve Sholes, Bob Wills, Gene Autry, Original Carter Family, Arthur Satherley, Jimmie Davis, and The Orginal Sons Of The Pioneers. 24 songs: Peace In The Valley • Ashes Of Love • San Antonio Rose • Tumbling Tumble Weeds • Born To Lose • Worried Man's Blues • many more.
_____00359508    $8.95

**Volume 4**
Features: Chet Atkins, Patsy Cline, Owen Bradley, Kitty Wells, Hank Snow, Hubert Long, Connie B. Gay and Lefty Frizzell. Song highlights: Crazy • I'm Sorry • Making Believe • Wings Of A Dove • Saginaw, Michigan • and 16 others.
_____00359509    $8.95

**Volume 5**
Includes: Merle Travis, Johnny Cash, Grant Turner, Vernon Dalhart, Marty Robbins, Roy Horton, "Little" Jimmie Dickens. 19 selections: Sixteen Tons • Folsom Prison Blues • El Paso • Mockingbird Hill • May The Bird of Paradise.
_____00359512    $7.95

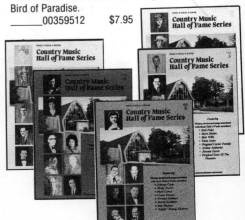

**HL Hal Leonard Publishing Corporation**
For more information, see your local music dealer, or write to:
P.O. Box 13819  Milwaukee, Wisconsin 53213